101 Amazing Things to Do in Taiwan

© 2018 101 Coolest Things

All rights reserved. No part of this publication may be reproduced, distributed, or transmitted in any form or by any means, including photocopying, recording, or other electronic or mechanical methods, without the prior written permission of the publisher, except in the case of brief quotations embodied in critical reviews and certain other noncommercial uses permitted by copyright law.

Introduction

So you're going to Taiwan huh? You are very very lucky indeed! You are sure in for a treat because Taiwan is an underrated and relatively unexplored gem of Asia that offers ever visitor a magical experience.

This guide will take you on a journey from the major cities like Taipei, through to the coastal regions, the various islands, and the national parks too.

In this guide, we'll be giving you the low down on:
- the very best things to shove in your pie hole, from incredible street market eats like stinky tofu and egg pudding to some of the craziest themed restaurants around the country
- incredible festivals, whether you would like to party hard by the beach or you want to join in with the Chinese New Year celebrations
- the coolest historical and cultural sights that you simply cannot afford to miss from museums where you can learn how to make paper through to a pre-historic site that's 5000 years old

- the most incredible outdoor adventures, whether you want to ride the waves of Penghu Island, or you fancy white water rafting on the rapids of a local river
- the places where you can party like a local and make new friends
- and tonnes more coolness besides!

Let's not waste any more time – here are the 101 most amazing, spectacular, and cool things not to miss in Taiwan!

1. Eat Egg Pudding From Jiufen Bus Station

There is certainly no shortage of incredible things to eat in Taiwan, but you won't always find deliciousness in fancy restaurants but in much stranger places indeed. Take Jiufen bus station, for example. This is a bustling place for commuters in Taipei city, but it's also a place to chow down on delicious snacks like Taiwanese egg pudding. This is essentially a kind of silky egg custard that the local people love, but the difference with this place is you have the opportunity to eat it right out of the shell.

2. Watch Taiwanese Opera at the National Taichung Theatre

Although Taiwan is a small island nation, it does have its own form of culture that you can't find anywhere else. If you would like a cultural experience that is uniquely Taiwanese, be sure to head to the National Taichung Theatre, which often showcases Taiwanese opera, the only form of drama native to Taiwan. These performances typically tell old Taiwanese folk tales that are very dear to the hearts of the local population.
(No. 101, Section 2, Huilai Rd, Xitun District, Taichung City; http://en.npac-ntt.org)

3. Be Blown Away by Sand Sculptures in Fulong

Many people head to the south of Taiwan when they want to visit a beach, but actually there are great beaches that are just a stone's throw away from Taipei City. Fulong is one such getaway that's immensely popular with locals. This is a great beach to visit at any time of the year, but it truly comes to life during the Fulong Sand Sculpture Festival, which is held from May to July. The sand sculptures show the talents of local people, and are truly astounding.

(www.eventaiwan.tw/cal_en/cal_20018)

4. Eat Oyster Omelettes From the Street

If you ever eat oysters at home, you probably consider the experience to be something reserved for a special occasion, but in Taiwan oysters are abundant and it's easy to find them everywhere that you go. They are particularly popular when fried up into an omelette. The combination of fluffy eggs mixed with tapioca and then chewy fresh oysters is something that is always satisfying.

5. Be Stunned by the Qingshui Cliff

As an island nation, there is so much stunning coastline to take in on a trip to Taiwan that it's hardly doable in one vacation away, but one spot of dramatic coastline that you absolutely should not miss is the Qingshui Cliff. This dramatic cliff face has been designated one of the eight wonders of Taiwan, and its height of 1000 metres and sheer vertical drop make it a very imposing sight indeed. From the cliffs, you also have a majestic view of all the colours of the ocean.

6. Visit the Birthplace of Bubble Tea, Chun Shui Tang

When it's a hot day and you cool yourself down with a refreshing glass of bubble tea, have you ever wondered where this wondrous creation started? Well, it's actually something Taiwanese, and you can go straight to the source in Taipei by visiting Chun Shui Tang, the very place that invented the drink. For us, the bubble tea there is perfect. It's sweet but not overly so, it has a strong tea flavour, and the tapioca balls are the perfect balance between soft and chewy.

(No. 21之1號, Zhongshan S Rd, Zhongzheng District, Taipei City; http://chunshuitang.com.tw)

7. Experience the Hungry Ghost Festival

The seventh month of the lunar calendar in Taiwan is better known as Ghost Month. This is when the gates of hell are opened and an army of hungry ghosts come to the earth to haunt the living and eat Taiwanese food (of course). During this month, you can have the local experience by visiting your nearest temple, burning some incense, and asking for protection. One thing you should never do during this month is actually say the word "ghost" because legend has it that this will invoke the spirits and attract them to you.

8. Have a Skiing Adventure Mt Hehuan

When you think of destinations around the world for a skiing or snow boarding adventure, it's unlikely that Taiwan would be a place that springs to mind, but actually Taiwan is a country that experiences all four seasons, and there are high enough mountains to get a decent amount of snow in the winter months. Although Mt Hehuan isn't the tallest mountain in Taiwan, it has the best snowfall and it's where you want to be if you want to enjoy winter sports.

9. Indulge in the Taiwanese Mega-Dumpling, Ba Wan

Dumplings might just be the ultimate comfort food, and Taiwan might have created the dumpling of all dumplings, something called Ba Wan. These dumplings are typically around 6-8cm in diameter, which makes them significantly larger than your average, and on a day when you're not super hungry, one of these would be sufficient for a lunch. The dumpling will typically be filled with pork, bamboo shoots, and mushrooms, and then covered in a sweet and sour sauce.

10. Ride the Maokong Gondola

Taipei is a city with an incredible transport system that makes it easy to get around. But actually, the transport in the city is more than just a way from getting from A to B – it's a tourist attraction in its own right. The Maokong Gondola is a cable car or air gondola form of transportation that only has four stops, and takes passengers from Taipei Zoo to Maokong, which is a mountainous part of Taipei with stunning tea plantations and teahouses.

(http://english.gondola.taipei)

11. Watch the Fireflies of Carp Pond

Carp Pond is the third largest lake in the Hualien area, and it's the kind of place you go to get away from it all and let life's responsibilities slide from your shoulders. While there is certainly no bad time of the year to visit Carp Pond, it's at its most magical from April to June, which is firefly season. At this time, you will see the fireflies light up the landscape above and around you.

12. Shop for Souvenirs at Ata Aboriginal Culture Craft

Before you leave Taiwan, you'll almost certainly want to stock up on some cool souvenirs that will enable you to always remember this incredible country. Trust us when we tell you to bypass the cheesy souvenir shops, and instead make a stop at Ata Aboriginal Culture Craft in

Taitung City where you can purchase handcrafted Taiwanese aboriginal items such as textiles, jewellery, and leather work.

(No.7, Ln. 200, Sec. 2, Zhongxing Rd; Taitung)

13. Be Wowed by the Golden Waterfall

Taiwan is a country that has it all. The epic cities provide dynamic cultural opportunities, but there's also plenty of space for incredible landscapes. If you want to discover natural Taiwan, we think that the Golden Waterfall is something that will blow you away. This waterfall is pretty easy to get to as it exists in the popular Jiufen area that tourists love. The water here gushes over red rocks, and it's best to visit in the rainy season when the water flow is the strongest.

14. Have an Artsy Day at the Taipei Fine Arts Museum

When you think of arts focused countries around the world, Taiwan might not be the first country that pops into your head, but in spite of this it's certainly possible for arty types to have a fantastic time in Taiwan, and particularly at the Taipei Fine Arts Museum. This museum is dedicated to modern art, with a strong focus on local Taiwanese artists. At night, coloured lights are projected on to the building, providing a very beautiful nightscape. *(No. 181, Section 3, Zhongshan N Rd, Zhongshan District, Taipei City; www.tfam.museum)*

15. Have the Taiwanese Hot Pot Experience

Although Taiwan is very hot in the summer time, there is quite the contrast in the winter months, and if you do visit in the colder time of year, you'll be in need of a winter jacket and some warming, comfort food. Well, it doesn't get much warmer or more comforting than a traditional Taiwanese hot pot. Hot pots are great sharing food, and in Taiwan everything is thrown into the pot – thin slices of meat, seafood, cubes of fried tofu, and veggies! The difference with the Taiwanese version is that you also get to enjoy a spicy dipping sauce on the side.

16. Hike to the Top of KeeLung Mountain

For people who are not accustomed to bustling cities, Taipei can be quite the shock. But when it all gets too much, there are plenty of day trips that you can take to experience some fresh air outside of the city. Jiufen is an area just outside of the city that is home to the magnificent KeeLung Mountain. The mountain is 588 metres tall, and there are stone steps that can take you all the way to the top. Be sure to set off early to avoid the midday sun.

17. Say Hi to the Animals at Taipei Zoo

If you are an animal lover, visiting a zoo is always a point of contention. Yes, it's great to see the animals up close, but not all zoos perform ethically. Fortunately, with Taipei Zoo you have nothing to worry about because it's one of the leading zoological institutions for conservation, research, and education. It also happens to be the largest zoo in Asia so there is tonnes to see. The Giant Panda House is, however, the highlight for most people, and to see these endangered animals up close and living happily is a real treat.

(No. 30, Section 2, Xinguang Rd, Wenshan District, Taipei City; http://english.zoo.gov.taipei)

18. Release a Sky Lantern at Shifen

Taipei is a very large city, and when visiting you shouldn't restrict yourself to the centre of the city, because much of the charm lies in outlying districts. Take Shifen, for example. This is an old railroad town on the edge of Taipei that can give you a glimpse into how the big city used to be many years ago. Something really fun to do here is release a paper lantern into the sky. You can write your wishes on the lantern, and then set it free on the wind.

19. Feel the Breadth of History at the National Palace Museum

For history buffs in Taiwan, there is nowhere that's quite as impressive as the National Palace Museum in Taipei, which has around 700,000 ancient Chinese imperial artefacts and artworks, which is one of the largest collections of this type anywhere in the world. It's more than possible to spend a few days here. You can explore Chinese paintings from the Tang Dynasty, rare ceramics created for the Song Dynasty, Ding Porcelain, rare books from the Ming Dynasty, and lots more besides.

(No. 221, Section 2, Zhishan Rd, Shilin District, Taipei City; www.npm.gov.tw/en)

20. Treat Yourself to a Taiwanese Foot Massage

Taiwan is a great country for walking around and seeing the incredible sights on foot, but at the end of a long day of sightseeing, your feet will be feeling a little bit worse for wear. Fortunately, this is when a Taiwanese foot massage can save the day. A Taiwanese foot massage is harder than your average, and some people can even find it a little bit painful. But afterwards, your feet will be totally renewed and ready for lots of more walking action around Taiwan.

21. Eat at a Restaurant With a Difference in Taichung

Taiwan is a country with a very vibrant food culture, but sometimes it's the surroundings of where you eat that make the experience more special than the food itself. That will certainly be the case if you visit Carton Kind in Taichung city. The unique selling point here is that virtually everything inside the restaurant is made from paper. Your cutlery is paper, your bowls and plates are paper (and can even be washed up), and you'll even sit on paper chairs.

(No. 1, Lane 281, Section 3, Xitun Road, Xitun District, Taichung City)

22. Learn About Taiwanese Pottery in Yingge

There are numerous towns dotted around Taipei that are great for showcasing a more traditional way of local life, or a particular skill, and Yingge is one of those towns, located just half an hour outside of the city. This town is well known for its incredible ceramics culture. Ceramics Old Street is a street lined with traditional ceramics shops, and they're a great place to find something special to take home. Some of these shops even host classes so you can have a spin of the potter's wheel.

23. Stay on a Working Flower Farm

During your time in Taiwan, you'll probably be staying in a selection of hotels, guesthouses, and hostels. While there's certainly a number of great accommodation options across the country, what if you'd prefer something out of the ordinary? Well, how about staying on a working flower farm? You can do exactly that at the Hua Lu Flower Leisure Farm. The owners grow the flowers to make their own essential oils, and as you can probably imagine, the whole place smells heavenly.

(No.43-3, Xiping, Zhuolan Township, Miaoli County 369)

24. Learn About Indigenous Taiwan

If you are a fan of museums, there's no doubt that you will have the National Palace Museum on your must-visit list in Taipei. Well, just opposite this museum is a lesser known but brilliant museum called the Shung Ye Museum of Formosan Aborigines. Although you wouldn't realise it from walking the streets of Taipei, there are 14 indigenous tribes from Taiwan, and this museum details their beliefs, festivals, geographic divisions, dress, agriculture, and art. *(No. 282, Section 2, Zhishan Rd, Shilin District, Taipei City; www.museum.org.tw/symm_en/01.htm)*

25. Watch the Changing of the Guards at Sun Yat-Sen Memorial Hall

Built in 1971, the Sun Yat-Sen Memorial Hall was created as a way to celebrate the life and commemorate the death of the Republic of China's founding father. Inside, you can find memorabilia about his life, and even attend grand concerts, but something that you can do totally for free is watch the changing of the guards, which takes place outside the building at the top of every hour.

(No. 505, Section 4, Ren'ai Rd, Xinyi District, Taipei City; www.yatsen.gov.tw/en/)

26. Dip in the World's Only Saltwater Hot Spring

For perfect days of endless relaxation, Green Island is definitely the place to be. Not only is the island absolutely stunning with an array of beaches that are second to none, this island is also home to the world's one and only saltwater hot spring. Throughout the year, the water is an ideal temperature that fluctuates between 60 and 70 degrees, making it perfect for long bathing. The water comes from the sea, and underground water that is heated by volcanic lava on the island.

27. Learn About Local Wines at Taichung Winery

Taiwan is certainly not a country that is greatly famed for its wine production, but if you can't resist a glass or two, we don't think that Taiwan will disappoint you at all, and one place you shouldn't miss on your itinerary is the

Taichung Winery. Lucky for you, it's possible to take a tour of the whole place where you can better understand the manufacturing process, see the winery gardens, and, of course, sample the product.

(No. 2, Industrial 28th Rd, Situn District, Taichung City)

28. Cycle the Dongfeng Green Bikeway

Cycling is something that is promoted greatly by the Taiwanese government, and this means that there are many well established cycle paths of visitors who love nothing more than to put their feet to the pedal. The Dongfeng Green Bikeway is an enduringly popular cycle path that extends for a very pleasant 13 kilometres. Riding is very safe because no cars are allowed, and you'll see disused railways, gushing rivers, beautiful foliage, local farmlands, and more besides.

29. Have a Day of Learning at the National Museum of History

For history buffs on a trip to Taiwan, the National Museum of History in Taipei is an absolute must visit place. This museum opened in 1955, and since then its

collection of artefacts pertaining to the history of Taiwan and mainland China has grown exponentially. Inside, you'll find items from the Neolithic period, ancient Chinese dynasties, and the contemporary period as well, with objects like precious jade, bronze carvings, historic documents, and more besides.
(No. 49, Nanhai Rd, Zhongzheng District, Taipei City; www.nmh.gov.tw/en/index.htm)

30. Visit an Historic Dutch Fortress in Tainan

When you think of Taiwan, you probably think of a dynamic city with bustling cities, but if you look hard enough you can also get a picture of Taiwan in the centuries gone by. Take Anping Fort, formally known as Fort Zeelandia, for example. The fort can be found in the city of Tainan, and was built over a 10 year period, from 1924 to 1934, by the Dutch East India Company. This was a very important place for connecting trade between Europe and Asia in the seventeenth century.
(No. 82, Guosheng Rd, Anping District, Tainan City)

31. Boat Through the Mangrove Swamps of Taijiang National Park

Taijiang National Park in the southwest of Taiwan is an area of huge national importance to the local people because it's here that the first settlers landed in the country. Historical significance aside, this national park is a wonderful place to get back to nature, and to experience its tidal flats, lagoons, and mangrove swamps. It's possible to book guides inside the park who will take you on boat trips through those mangrove swamps, which is a wonderful way to get to know a less explored part of Taiwan.

(No. 118, Sicao Blvd, Annan District, Tainan City; www.tjnp.gov.tw/Eng)

32. Party Hard at the Spring Scream Festival

When you think of places around the world that offer incredible music festivals, Taiwan might not be a country at the top of your list, but if you love to party, you love music, and you love the outdoors, the annual Spring Scream Festival that is hosted in the country's Kenting National Park could be something that appeals to you.

With seven music stages, and over 250 bands and DJs performing, there is something for everyone. *(https://springscream.com)*

33. Explore One of Taiwan's Oldest Town's, Daxi

The Daxi township, which is actually a part of Taoyuan City, is one of the oldest parts of Taiwan, and it's well worth a visit for its cute streets and historic feel. Daxi was a very important town for trade in the 19th century. These days, not so much, and it's very quiet, but if you want to take it easy and check out old fashioned Taiwan, it's a great place to be. Visit the Old Street Market, and you can pick up many treats to eat and take home with you.

34. Unwind in the Hot Springs of Beitou

What can possibly be more relaxing than finding natural hot springs where you can relax your weary muscles? Well, fortunately the popular Beitou hot springs can be located on the outskirts of Taipei city, so they are the perfect day trip when you feel drained from city life. Dating way back to the times of Japanese colonial rule, Beitou was then actually one of the largest hot spring complexes anywhere in the world.

35. Sing Your Heart Out at Karaoke Bars

If you really want to enjoy some evening entertainment just like a true Taiwanese person, one of the best things you can do is grab a microphone and sing your heart out at a karaoke bar, mostly known as KTVs in Taiwan, which are hugely popular across the country, but particularly in the big cities. One of the most popular KTV joints is called Cashbox KTV, and you can find it close to Ximending MRT station in Taipei city. It operates 24 hours a day 365 days a year, so you have no excuse.
(No. 22號, Section 4, Zhongxiao E Rd, Da'an District, Taipei City)

36. Visit the World's Largest Stained Glass Installation

The transport system in Taiwan is very impressive indeed, and you'll have no problem getting from place to place using the high speed trains. But it's not just the trains but also the train stations in Taiwan that are impressive. In the

Kaohsiung MRT station, you can find something called the Dome of Light, a public art installation made from coloured glass that covers an area of 660 square metres and was created by Italian artist Narcissus Quagliata.

37. Get to Grips With Buddhism in Taiwan

On the busy streets of Taipei you'd never guess it, but Taiwan can also be a great place to relax. And if you need some Buddhist calm in your life, the place to visit would definitely be Fo Guang Shan Buddhist Memorial Monastery, located in Kaohsiung. Every other weekend, they have an open weekend, and you can go and visit, take part in meditation activities with practicing monks, as well as the chants and various monastic activities of the centre. *(No. 1, Tongling Road, Dashu District, Kaohsiung City; www.fgsbmc.org.tw/en)*

38. Wave a Rainbow Flag at Taipei Pride

If you are an LGBT traveller going to Taiwan for the first time and you don't have much of an idea of its gay culture, fear not because Taiwan is a very gay friendly place for travelling, and you can find this out for yourself if you

make it to the capital in time for Taipei Pride, which is hosted each year around the end of October. With 80,000 people from around the world in attendance, it's one of the largest and most celebratory Pride events to be found in Asia. Make sure you're there!
(www.twpride.org)

39. Dare to Try Pig's Blood Cake

If you love to try new food when you're in a different country, Taiwan has plenty for you to sample, and one of the most unique dishes of them all has to be pig's blood cake, a street food snack that can be found all over the country. In this snack, you'll find a mixture of pig's blood, sticky rice, and soy broth. This is then either fried or steamed and coated in peanut flour before being eaten.

40. Experience the Fun of the Dragon Boat Festival

When you visit Asia, the local festivals are a world apart from anything you will have experienced, and they're a great way of getting on board with local culture. The Dragon Boat Festival is definitely one of our favourites.

This festival is a commemoration of a legendary scholar called Cyu Yuan. When he died, he jumped into the river, and boats trawled up and down the river to find his body. This is the origin of the dragon boat race, and it's celebrated in many places across Taiwan.

41. Take a Boat Tour Around Sun Moon Lake

Sun Moon Lake is the largest body of water to be found anywhere in Taiwan, and a wonderfully peaceful place to visit if you want to chill out and take it easy. Because the expanse of water is so large, we think it's a very good idea to take a boat tour of the lake. With a boat tour, you get to visit an isolated island in the middle of the water called Lalo, where a Taiwanese indigenous tribe lives.

42. Spot Whales in Hualien

Taiwan is an island surrounded by water, and that means that you can have just as many incredible experiences on the water itself as you can on mainland Taiwan. Something that you might want to try in the Hualien area is a whale watching tour. In these waters, there are 29 different species of whales and dolphins, including humpback whales, killer whales, and sperm whales, so there is a very good chance you'll see something extra special out there on the water.

43. Pass an Evening at Shilin Night Market

Market culture is a massive deal in Taiwan. The markets across the country are not just places where you can find cheap things to eat, but are vibrant social hubs. Many of the markets take place at night, and young people meet there like they would at a bar or restaurant. Probably the most famous market in the country is Taipei's Shilin night market. With 539 stalls, this is a shopper's and eater's paradise.

(Lane 101, Wenlin Rd, Shilin District, Taipei City; www.shilin-night-market.com)

44. Walk the Winding Streets of Lukang

Taiwan is a small island, but in spite of this there are many hidden surprises that you can find all around the country, and one of our favourite "off the beaten tracks" spots is a township called Lukang. The town is well known for its curiously winding streets, its handicrafts, and for being home to the most beautiful temples in all of Taiwan. The Matsu Temple is a must visit place in Lukang, and is home to incredible stone carvings and old Chinese paintings and calligraphy.

45. Visit the 921 Earthquake Museum of Taiwan

On September 21st of 1999, Taiwan experienced a 7.3 magnitude earthquake that devastated parts of the country such as Nantou and Taichung counties, took the lives of more than 2500 people, and destroyed the local economy. It's a sombre place to visit, but the 921 Earthquake Museum of Taiwan is also a great place to learn about earthquakes and this particular time in the country's history. It can be found in Kengkou village in Taichung County.

(No.46, Zhongzheng Rd., Kengkou Village, Wufeng District, Taichung City; www.921emt.edu.tw)

46. Hike the Dakeng Scenic Area

For nature lovers, there's plenty to explore across Taiwan, and one of the most magical places for scenes of natural beauty is the Dakeng Scenic Area, which lies just outside of Taichung city. For hikers, this place is total magic because there are ten well marked hiking trails you can take with no need for a guide. Trails 1 to 5 are for people who want daring mountainous hikes, and 6 to 10 are closer to the city and not quite as challenging.

47. Try the Taiwanese Hamburger, Gua Bao

When you're in a new country for the first time, you want to try lots of new food, but sometimes all you want to eat is a juicy burger. Well in Taiwan you can have the best of both worlds because the country has its very own variation on a burger called Gua Bao. This dish consists of a light and fluffy steamed bun which is typically filled with a stewed pork mixture, pickled mustard, coriander, and ground peanuts. Honestly, these might be better than burgers as you know them.

48. Join in the Fun of the Mazu Pilgrimage Festival

On any visit to Taiwan, you need to know about Mazu. Mazu is the Chinese patron goddess who is said to protect seafarers, fishermen, and sailors, something that is obviously very important to an island nation. Well, it's possible to pay your own respects to Mazu at the annual Mazu Pilgrimage Festival, which involves an eight day holy pilgrimage from Zhenlan Temple in Dajia to Fentian Temple in Xingang.

49. Have an Artsy Day at the National Taiwan Museum of Fine Arts

There are some awesome museums in Taiwan, and it's not the case that all of the best ones are found in the capital city. For artsy types, we think that the National Taiwan Museum of Fine Arts, which can be found in Taichung city, is definitely one of the most impressive in the country. This is an incredible place to get to grips with the breadth of Taiwanese art, with 16 galleries containing contemporary art. The sculpture garden is also a fantastic place for an art-filled stroll on a sunny day.
(No. 2, Section 1, Wuquan West Road, West District, Taichung City; http://english.ntmofa.gov.tw/English)

50. Get Back to Nature in Taipei Botanical Garden

With over 2.5 million inhabitants, Taipei is the kind of place that can easily become overwhelming for those unaccustomed to city ways, but a great place you can always escape to is the Taipei Botanical Garden. Covering 15 acres and playing host to 1500 plant species, this is the number one place in the city to get back to nature. Some of the highlights include a lotus pond, a fern garden, and a succulent plants garden.

(No. 53, Nanhai Rd, Zhongzheng District, Taipei City; http://tpbg.tfri.gov.tw/en/Introduction.php)

51. Explore an Important Archaeological Site, Beinan Park

When you think of countries you'd visit to see sites of archaeological importance, you'd probably be inclined to go to Greece or Cambodia, but Taiwan also plays host to some ancient history, and you can discover it in Beinan Park, which can be found in Taitung county. This is the site of the largest prehistoric settlement that's been found in Taiwan thus far. This is primarily a burial site, and it dates back an astonishing 5000 years.

52. Eat Pepper Buns at the Raohe Night Market

Although Taiwan is not an especially large country, you will definitely notice some differences in the cuisines as you travel from place to place. In fact, there are even some markets that have their own typical foods, and something you'll want to seek out at Raohe Night Market in Taipei are the pepper buns. These are essentially the pork buns that you can find in many places in Asia, but they are also filled with lots of black pepper, and the spicy taste really comes through.

(Raohe St, Songshan District, Taipei City)

53. Feel Taiwan's Religious History at Longshan Temple

When people set foot in Taipei for the first time, they often think of it as a dynamic, contemporary city, but this is only one side of the story. There are also important temples around Taipei, and the most important of them all is the Longshan Temple, which was built way back in 1738. The temple is particularly interesting because it mixes Confucian, Taoist, and Buddhist design. Its roof with dragon and phoenix creatures is very striking.

(No. 211, Guangzhou St, Wanhua District, Taipei City; http://lungshan.org.tw/en/index.php)

54. Stroll Qixingtan Beach on a Sunny Day

In our opinion, one of the most severely underrated beaches in Taiwan is Qixingtan beach. Yes, it's true that this is a pebble beach rather than a sandy beach so sunbathing might not be on the agenda, but this doesn't prevent it from being a site of incredible natural beauty. There are many sightseeing trails along the beach and by the coast so you can easily check out the area on foot, and there's even a stargazing pavilion for the night time.

55. Watch a Taiwanese Puppet Show in Yunlin

If you make it to the south-west of the country, there is a town called Yunlin that's well worth a visit. As well as serving up delicious hard clams, this is the place that Taiwanese puppet theatre originated in the country, and this is a source of great pride for many of the local people. The Yunlin Puppet Theatre Museum is a place where you can learn about this artistic tradition, and also catch live performances.

(No. 498, Section 1, Linsen Rd, Huwei Township, Yunlin County)

56. Eat Incredible French Food in Taichung City

Look, we know that you didn't go all the way to Taiwan to eat French food, but there is a restaurant called Le Mout in Taichung City that was recently voted the 26th best restaurant in Asia, and that's a good enough of a reason to book a table as any. And the food is French with a Taiwanese twist so you won't be completely immersed in fancy European fare. Imagine duck egg with chestnut porridge and garlic-almond crumbles – delicious!
(No. 59, Cunzhong St, West District, Taichung City; www.lemout.com)

57. Admire the Colours of the Yinyang Sea

If you happen to visit the Gold Ecological Park in the north part of the country, it's well worth making a short diversion and checking out the Yinyang Sea at the same time. This is a patch of ocean, which when viewed at a distance, appears to have blue and yellow patches that swirl together. These contrasting elements are reflected in the Yin and Yang concept that are popular in Asian culture.

58. Pass an Afternoon at the Miniatures Museum of Taiwan

One of the cutest and most unique museums in Taipei has to be the Miniatures Museum of Taiwan. As you step inside, you will suddenly feel like a giant, when in reality it's everything around you that will have shrunk. Some of the things you will find inside include miniature doll's houses, great works of architecture in miniature, and scenes from magical fairy tales. A great place to keep kids entertained.

(96 Jianguo N Rd, Sec 1, Taipei; www.mmot.com.tw)

59. Join in The Fun of the Pingxi Sky Lantern Festival

The Sky Lantern Festival is a Chinese festival that started in the Xing dynasty, and it's celebrated in many parts of Asia, but if you want to celebrate in Taiwan, the place to be is Pingxi. The time of the festival changes each year, but it's typically celebrated during February or in early

March. The basic idea is that you purchase a lantern, you scribble your desires, hopes, and ambitions on it, and then release it into the sky alongside thousands of other lanterns in the hope that your dreams will come true.

60. Snack on Handmade Fish Balls

If you really want to have a local experience while you're in Taiwan, it's important to eat like a local and expanding your mind and palette in the process. Something that's very popular right across Asia is the fish ball. These can be put in soups or simply grilled on a stick. But the style in Taiwan is slightly different to other parts of Asia. The local vendors put more air into the ball. This means they soak up more stock when put in a soup, and that they're chewier when grilled.

61. Party the Night Away at Club Myst

Since Taipei is a happening capital city with a vibrant youth culture, there's more than a handful of places to party the night away. If your idea of a good time is moving your feet to banging music until break of dawn, Club Myst is a place in the capital that might just grab your interest.

Club Myst is open absolutely every night of the week, and with its variety of rooms, stages, and podiums, you'll never be bored there.
(9F, ATT4Fun, No. 12, Song Shou Rd. Taipei; www.clubmyst.com)

62. Ride the Waves of Penghu Island

Although Taiwan is an island itself, there are also many islands dotted around the mainland, and these are a must visit for anybody with any kind of beach fever. Penghu Island is particularly lovely, with one of Taiwan's oldest temples that dates back more than 375 years. But beyond the culture, there's also an incredible surfing culture here. There are quite a few surf schools that can guide you through the watersport from a beginners' level, so why not give it a shot?

63. Celebrate Chinese New Year Like a Local

Chinese New Year is a huge deal in Taiwan, and if you happen to be in Taiwan during February for this celebration, you are in for one hell of a party. There are many aspects to the holiday such as giving money in a red envelope to family, but for non-locals, you can still join in with the parties. At this time of year, there will be tonnes of revellers around Sun Moon Lake, so if you want a mixture of nature and partying, that would be a great place to be.

64. Find Something Special at Art Tapei

True art lovers visiting Taiwan need to know about Art Taipei. This annual art show is hosted in October each year, and visiting not only gives you the opportunity to check out the creative talent of local Taiwanese artists, but you can also take home some artwork for your own humble abode. If you want to take something home with you that is truly original, a visit to the Art Taipei is certainly worth the effort.

(http://art-taipei.com)

65. Take a Dip at the Sun Moon Lake Swimming Carnival

The Sun Moon Lake is an enduringly popular place for locals and tourists alike to chill out and relax, but there's one time of year when the lake becomes a frenzy of activity, and that's during the Sun Moon Lake swimming carnival, which is held at the beginning of August each year. The highlight is a 3km swimming race, which thousands of people take part in. And if swimming isn't your thing, you can cheer on the racers while enjoying the fireworks, laser shows, and live concerts.

66. Chow Down on Stinky Tofu

Taiwan is a food lover's paradise, but you might think twice about putting some of the most popular Taiwanese dishes into your mouth. Stinky tofu is one such example. This street food doesn't sound all that appealing, and when it's described, it often doesn't appeal all that much either. Stinky tofu is basically tofu that has been fermented, and the local say the stinkier the better. You'll find this at every Taiwanese night market.

67. Chill on the Beaches of Kenting National Park

As an island nation, Taiwan is surrounded by water, which is great news for all beach lovers who want to use their trip to the country as an opportunity to top up their tans.

Right at the southern tip of Taiwan you can find the Kenting National Park, which contains some of the most spectacular beaches in the country. We particularly like White Sand Bay because of its calm waters, and the opportunities for snorkelling and scuba diving that abound.
(www.ktnp.gov.tw/en)

68. Dance, Dance, Dance at the Ultra Music Festival

If you love nothing more than to dance to heavy beats and slick electronica, you need to know about Ultra Music Festival. This outdoor dance festival has many platforms around the world, it originated in Miami, and there is an annual event hosted in Taipei as well. Acts that have previously played at the festival include Afrojack, Armin Van Buuren, and Fedde le Grand.
(https://ww.ultramusicfestival.com)

69. Enjoy Coffee With a Difference at Gabee Coffee

If you are the sort of person who can't start their day until they have a cup of hot coffee inside them, you won't be alone on the streets of Taipei, because as well as bubble tea, coffee is hugely popular. There are numerous cafes you can visit for a steaming cup full of caffeine, but the place we heartily recommend is called Gabee Coffee. The quality of the coffee is second to none, but it's the beautiful and original latte art that keeps us coming back for more.

(No. 21, Lane 113, Section 3, Minsheng E Rd, Songshan District, Taipei City; www.gabee.cc)

70. Visit an Indigenous Village, Ita Thao

If you make it to the picturesque area of Sun Moon Lake, something you must do is visit a small village called Ita Thao. As well as being very pretty, this village is unique because it's home to a small indigenous group of people called the Thao. The Thao cultural village inside Ita Thao is a great place to learn about the people who live there, eat their food, listen to their music, and watch their dances.

71. Keep Kids Happy at the Taipei Children's Amusement Park

When you travel with kids, you want to give them memories that last a lifetime, but at the same time, it can be hard to keep kids entertained. Well, somewhere you should know about in the capital city is the Taipei Children's Amusement Park. There are 14 paid rides within the park, but tonnes of other stuff to keep the kids happy too, such as playgrounds, ball pits, and even hiking trails the whole family can enjoy.
(No. 55, Section 5, Chengde Rd, Shilin District, Taipei City; http://english.tcap.taipei)

72. Take in a Baseball Game at the National Stadium in Kaohsiung

If you are a sporty type, you might want to catch a live sports game on your trip to Taiwan. Because of the atmosphere of the crowd combined with the talent of the players, we think that a baseball game is the way to go, and the most impressive stadium is certainly the National Stadium, which you'll be able to find in Kaohsiung. The stadium has capacity for 55,000 spectators, and when it fills up the atmosphere is nothing short of electric.

(No. 100, Shiyun Blvd, Zuoying District, Kaohsiung City)

73. Be Mesmerised by Shifen Waterfall

If you find yourself in Taipei and a little overwhelmed by the hustle and bustle of the city, it can be a great idea to pay a visit to Shifen, a town on the outskirts that's very traditional, and even has its own waterfall. From the station, it only takes about 15 minutes to walk to the waterfall, and once you are there, you'll find the gushing water to be simply mesmerising. This is a very wide waterfall with a horse shoe shape.

74. Feel Taipei's Creativity at Songshan Cultural & Creative Park

Taipei is a city with an incredible creative pulse, and this can be felt at the Songshan Cultural & Creative Park more than anywhere else in the city. This complex of buildings has so much to offer, you'll return again and again. There are independent shops selling wares from local designers, there's a baroque garden where banquets and fashion events are hosted, you'll find a design museum, performance spaces, and lots more exciting stuff besides.

75. Get Close to the Cats of Houtong Cat Village

These days, it seems like you can't open social media without seeing a cat meme or a funny cat video. The world is positively cat crazy, and if you love cats a whole lot, we think you might never want to leave Houtoung Cat Village, which as the name would suggest, is a place that's absolutely swarming with feline friends. And more than just cats, you'll find cat sculptures, a cat themed walkway, and even cafes serving up cat shaped food.

76. Eat Snake Meat at the Snake Alley Night Market

Snake Alley, which is more formally known as Huaxi Night Market, is not just a cute name. This is a place where you can actually eat snake meat. There are many different ways that snake meat is served up, and eating there could be quite the experience. You could purchase snake as a kind of medicine, you could have it infused into wine, you could slurp up a bowlful of snake soup, or you could even drink snake blood like a shot.

(Huaxi St, Wanhua District, Taipei City)

77. Go Back in Time at the Museum of Prehistory

While Taiwan might not be a country that's especially well known for its long history, history buffs aren't left out on a trip to the country if they pay a visit to the very well curated National Museum of Prehistory in Taitung City. At the museum, you will learn about the geological birth of the country, the various stages of Taiwan's history, and you'll even learn about the indigenous people's rights movement. Don't miss it.

(1 Museum Road, Taitung; http://en.nmp.gov.tw)

78. Explore the Extraordinary Landscapes of Yehliu Geopark

Yehliu Geopark is one of the most unique places on the face of the planet, and a must visit when you are in northern Taiwan. Yehliu is actually a cape that extends for 1700 metres, and has been formed by Datun Mountain extending out into the sea. Because of the quality of the rock and the sea erosion, there's a number of strange rock formations with huge rocks that look like candles or pots and pans.

(www.ylgeopark.org.tw/eng/info/ylintroduction_en.aspx)

79. Have a Local Experience With Couchsurfing

Staying in a hostel is a really great idea for when you want to meet other backpackers and find some other travel buddies in Taiwan, but what if you actually want to have a more local experience? Then you need to know about courchsurfing.com. The basic premise of the website is that you can find local people in Taiwan (and all over the world!) who have a spare bed or a spare couch, and can put you up for a couple of nights. Yes it's money saving, but the true value comes with the incredible cultural exchange.
(www.couchsurfing.com)

80. Watch the Sunset at Tamsui Fisherman's Wharf

It's true that Taipei is a lively city, but there's also some very charming spots dotted around the city where you can relax with a cup of tea and take in the view. We think that Tamsui Fisherman's Wharf, located where the Tamsui river meets the sea, might just be the best of these spots.

The wharf really comes to life in the early evening because it's a fantastic place to take an alfresco dinner while breathing in some sea air and watching the sun set over Taipei.

81. Cool Down With a Mountain of Shaved Ice

In Taiwan's summertime, the temperatures can be positively sweltering, and you'll want to do everything that you can to cool off from the intense heat and humidity. In our opinion, there is no better way of doing this than by ordering up a mountain of shaved ice, a sweet treat that is commonly enjoyed by the local people. In Taiwan, this is known as baobing, and the ice is typically drenched in syrup, and toppings such as fruits, sprinkles, and even sweetened beans are added.

82. Trek the Caoling Historic Trail

For a mix of both culture and nature, you can't beat a day hiking the Caoling Historic Trail. This route extends from a town called Yuanwangkeng and goes down to Dali on the coast. As you walk along, you will find two huge Qing dynasty boulders that have ancient inscriptions on them, as well as some absolutely incredible nature, with trees, farmland, and mountains all around you as you walk.

83. Enjoy Drinks With a View at WET Bar

Taipei is the kind of cool city that provides numerous watering holes and awesome places to drink a cocktail or two. So many, in fact, that you might have trouble choosing. So trust us when we tell you to head straight for WET bar, which is a stylish rooftop bar on the top of the swanky W Taipei hotel. There is a pool on the rooftop deck so you can top up your tan and check out the view while having a few decadent rooftop drinks.

(No.10, Section 5, Zhongxiao East Road, Xinyi District, Taipei City; www.wtaipei.com/wetbar)

84. Chow Down at the Taipei International Beef Noodle Soup Festival

There are many people who travel all the way to Taipei simply to chow down on the incredible cuisine that the country has to offer, and something that's enduringly popular is beef noodle soup. But if you want to take your beef noodle soup experience to the next level and then some, you need to know about the Taipei International Beef Noodle Soup Festival. At the festival, awards are handed out to the best beef noodle soup chefs Oscars style.

85. Climb to the Top of Jade Mountain

For people who are really serious about hiking up mountains, Taiwan offers something very special indeed, Jade Mountain, which is also known as Yushan. This is the highest mountain on Taiwan, the fourth highest mountain on an island, and it has a height of 3952 metres above sea level. There are eleven mountain peaks on Jade Mountain, so you don't have to go all the way to the highest peak if you don't want to, but you should know that every one of the peaks is above 3000 metres.

86. Get Tipsy at the Taichung Wine & Spirit Festival

When you're on holiday, it can be great to relax with a few drinks, and if you'd like to sip on the best of what Taiwan has to offer, a trip to the Taichung Wine and Spirit Festival could be in order. The festival is held in mid July each year, and it's a great place to taste Taiwanese wines and other drinks. Because of the diverse landscape of Taiwan, it's actually a country that's surprisingly good at producing grapes for wine. And you can also try drinks like Taiwanese wine and sake.

87. Explore What's on Offer at Fengjia Night Market

Taichung is the third largest city in Taiwan, but with only 2 million people living there, it's not too overwhelming for people who can't deal with the hustle and bustle of places like Taipei. Of course, no trip to any Taiwanese city would be complete without visiting a night market, and the Fengjia Night Market is certainly the place to be in Taichung. Needless to say, the street food is a highlight. Don't leave without trying the octopus balls, the loaded baked potatoes, and the sweet taro ball soup.
(No. 440, Fuxing Rd, Xitun District, Taichung City)

88. Have a Diving Adventure on Green Island

If you love the ocean, you will love Taiwan, because it's in the waters of this island nation that you will experience some of the very best diving anywhere in Asia. Whether you're a diving first timer or an aficionado, the place to get your dive on is Green Island, which lies a 45 minute ferry ride away from Taitung city. With 600 species of fish, 150 species of reef building corals, and 50 species of soft coral, any experience under the waters of Green Island will be one to remember for a lifetime.

89. Make Paper at the Suho Memorial Paper Museum

The Suho Memorial Paper Museum is not the largest nor the best known museum in Taipei, but we think it's a very charming place to while away a dreary afternoon in the city. This museum is dedicated to paper craft. On the ground floor, you'll find a paper mill and very quaint gift shop, above that there are rotating exhibitions related to paper craft, and on the rooftop you can actually have a go at making paper yourself, and then relax in the rooftop teahouse.

(No.68, Section 2, Chang'an E Rd, Zhongshan District, Taipei City; www.suhopaper.org.tw/en/en_museum.html)

90. Enjoy a Day of Shopping on Dihua Street

If you love shopping but you'd rather avoid big shopping complexes for something altogether more charming, we can heartily recommend making your way to Dihua Street in Taipei. It was in the 1850s that this street was constructed, and these days the street is filled with shops selling Chinese medicine, a fabric market, and a New Year sundry market. Because of its charm, Dihua Street has also recently attracted quaint cafes and art studios.
(Dihua St, Datong District, Taipei City)

91. Snack on Iron Eggs

As you walk around the markets of Taiwan, there are going to be some foods that look very peculiar indeed, and iron eggs might just well be one of these. If you see eggs in miniature that are a deep black colour, you have found them. The eggs are repeatedly stewed until they become dark, flavourful, and chewy.

92. Have a Rafting Adventure on the Xiuguluan River

If you have something of an adventurous spirit, you might be interested in trying white water rafting on the rapids of the Xiuguluan River, which is the largest river in the east of Taiwan. The rafting distance is around 24 kilometres in length, and along that journey you will encounter an astounding twenty sets of rapids that takes around 3-4 hours to complete. There are tour companies that combine the rafting experience with camping and an outdoor barbecue for true adventurers.

93. Visit the Stone Temple of Kaohsiung

One of the most bizarre but beautiful sights in the whole country has to be the Stone Temple of Kaohsiung. Way back when, 500 migrant workers from southeast Asia were hired to create a motorway in the area. Unfortunately, the contractor went out of business, and the men were stranded with nothing. Fortunately a local temple took them in, and in return the workers built a magnificent temple adorned with sea shells, coral, and pieces of colourful stone.

(No. 2-7, Xinxing Rd, Tianliao District, Kaohsiung City)

94. Go Tea Crazy at the Ping-Lin Tea Museum

There is way more to the Taiwanese tea culture than bubble tea, and you can find this out for yourself on a trip to the Ping-Lin Tea Museum in Taipei city. The museum is comprised of three areas: tea history, tea making, and tea leaves. You'll learn about the tea plantations in the hills of Taiwan, and how tea culture has affected the whole country. The adjoining teahouse is, of course, a wonderful place for a hot cup of the good stuff.

(No.19-1, Shuisongqikeng, Shuide Village, Pinglin District, New Taipei City; http://en.tea.ntpc.gov.tw)

95. Eat From a Toilet Bowl at Modern Toilet

Taipei city truly has some of the most bonkers restaurants that we have experienced anywhere in the world, and a restaurant called Modern Toilet might just be at the top of that list. As the name would suggest, this is actually a toilet themed restaurant. As you walk into the restaurant, you could be mistaken for thinking you've stumbled into the restroom instead. And when your food arrives at the table it's actually served in a miniature toilet bowl.

(2F, No 7, Ln 50, Xinig S. Rd, Taipei; www.moderntoilet.com.tw/en/about.asp)

96. Experience the Phenomenon of Matsu Islands' Blue Tears

The Matsu Islands lie approximately 100km off the northwest coast of Taiwan, and they are a magical place to visit for one particular reason – this is the place where you can witness the natural phenomenon known as the "Blue Tears". What you will see when you visit are glowing blue waves that lap on to the shore. These are created by a particular type of glowing algae that is native to the Matsu Islands.

97. View the City from Taipei 101 Observatory

Taipei is a stunning city, but you can only really have a limited view of the city when you see it from the ground up. For an alternative view, it's a very good idea to make your way to the tallest observatory in the city, which can be found in the famous Taipei 101 building. The observatory is located almost 400 metres above the ground on the 89th floor of the building, and it's powered with high spec binoculars to get the best view of the whole city.

(No. 45, Shifu Rd., Xinyi District, Taipei City; www.taipei-101.com.tw)

98. Enjoy the Greenery of Da'an Forest Park

Every major city has a green space where locals and tourists can escape the honking of cars and chill out. New York has Central Park, London has Hyde Park, and Taipei has Da'an Forest Park. This expanse of green offers everything that you would expect from a city park: lots of grass and trees, paths that make running that much easier, a beautiful lake, and there is even an amphitheatre where you can catch local bands and orchestras.

(No.1, Section 2, Xinsheng South Road, Da'an District, Taipei City)

99. Experience the Beautiful Cherry Blossoms of Taiwan

You probably associate the cherry blossoms of spring time with Japan, but you can also spot these glorious blossoms in Taiwan, and in fact, there is an annual festival for just that called the Wulai Cherry Blossom Festival. Wulai is very accessible as it's only located about 40 minutes outside of central Tapei, and the mesmerising cherry blossoms that line the streets and the parks can be seen in February and March each year.

100. Shop With Local Youngsters in Ximending

Like any major city, Taipei is made up of lots of different districts, and each one of these has a different culture and something unique to offer. Ximending is one of the trendiest parts of Taipei, and if you want to go shopping like the young locals do, this is where you need to pound the pavement. Since this is a pedestrian zone, be sure to meander through the smaller alley ways, as this is where you can find street sellers offering some cool bargains, whether you're on the hunt for clothes, accessories, jewelleries, or something for your home.

101. Stroll Through the Aisles of the National Centre of Traditional Arts

On a visit to Taipei, you will have the impression that Taiwan is a buzzing and dynamic country. But that's only part of the story. Head to Yilan County and you can take in the more traditional side of Taiwan at the National

Centre of Traditional Arts. The museum is a great introduction to Taiwanese culture, but what makes it really stand out from the crowd are the live performances. Be sure to keep up with their schedule to catch a concert or dance performance.

(No. 201, Sec. 2, Wubin Rd., Wujie Township, Yilan County; http://en.ncfta.gov.tw)

Before You Go…

Thanks for reading **101 Amazing Things to Do in Taiwan.** We hope that it makes your trip a memorable one!

Have a great trip!
Team 101 Amazing Things